Childcraft

The How and Why Library

Volume 13

Look Again

Field Enterprises Educational Corporation

Chicago London Paris Rome Stuttgart Sydney Tokyo Toronto

Acknowledgments

The publishers of Childcraft—The How and Why Library
gratefully acknowledge the courtesy of the following
museums, publishers, photographers, and organizations.
Full illustration acknowledgments for this volume
appear with each reproduction or on page 283.

Curtis Publishing Company: photograph by John Lewis
Stage, page 53 (top), courtesy Holiday magazine,
copyright 1959 by The Curtis Publishing Company.

Bijutsu Shuppan-sha: photograph, page 250 (top),
copyright by Bijutsu Shuppan-sha, Tokyo.

The Frick Collection: paintings, pages 34 and 273,
copyright The Frick Collection, New York.

Toni Frissell: photograph, page 130, copyright by
Toni Frissell, 1955.

William Garnett: photographs, pages 128–129,
copyright by William Garnett.

Grandma Moses Properties, Inc.: painting, page 30,
copyright by Grandma Moses Properties, Inc., New
York.

Her Majesty the Queen, Elizabeth II: photograph, pages
144–145, copyright reserved.

Yousuf Karsh: photograph, page 270, copyright by
Yousuf Karsh.

Nationalmuseum, Stockholm: painting, page 99, copyright
by the Nationalmuseum, Stockholm.

New York Graphic Society Ltd.: photograph, page 116,
copyright by New York Graphic Society Ltd., Greenwich,
Conn.

Public Building Commission of Chicago: reproduction,
pages 278–279, copyright 1967 Public Building
Commission of Chicago. All rights reserved.

Smeets Lithographers: photograph, pages 102–103,
copyright by Smeets Lithographers, Weert, Netherlands.

Soho Gallery: photograph, pages 150–151, copyright
by Soho Gallery, London.

Time Inc.: photograph by Nina Leen, page 39, courtesy
Life magazine, copyright by Time Inc.; photograph
by Dmitri Kessel courtesy Life magazine, page 108,
copyright by Time Inc.; photograph by Carlo Bavagnoli
courtesy Life magazine, pages 168–169, copyright by
Time Inc.; photography, page 218 (left), courtesy of
Time-Life Books, copyright Time Inc.; photograph by
Eric Schall courtesy Time magazine, page 224, copyright
Time Inc. 1961.

Volume 13

Look Again

Contents

The More You Look, the More You See

When you look at a picture,
a statue—or anything—
you see it with your mind
as well as with your eyes.
Artists look at things
with their eyes and minds, too.
But they also look at things
with their imaginations.

Artists choose shapes and colors and sizes
from all the things they see.
They arrange them, and sometimes change them,
to make paintings or statues
or other kinds of art.

When you look at what an artist has made,
it can make you feel happy or sad.
It may puzzle you, or surprise you,
or make you laugh.
It may tell you things
about places and people—
even the artist who made it.

Artists and their works of art
can help you discover
how interesting many things can be.

Look at this photo
of the crowds, the rides,
and the side shows at a fair.
Enjoy the whole picture.
What do you see going on?

Now, turn the page.

If you pretend that you are an artist,
you might want to draw a picture
showing all that you see in the photo
you just looked at.
Or, in your drawing, you might want to show
just one part of the photo —
like this:

Or you might choose even smaller parts
that look like the ones on this page.

If you cut a hole in a sheet of paper
to make a small picture frame,
you can slide the frame around
on any big picture
to find little pictures that you like.

That is something like what an artist does.
He looks at the world, and then looks again
to find a picture.

Turn the page to see what some real artists
have painted of what they saw at a fair.

ou can see so much at a state fair
that you might wonder later
what you liked best.
Was it the ride,
as the horses whirled to the music
of the *carrousel* (merry-go-round)?
Or was it watching the strong man
lift a thousand pounds?
Artists who get ideas for paintings at fairs
show the color and the action.
And when you look at the paintings,
you remember the fun.
What pictures would you paint of a fair?

Carrousel by Paula Algminowicz.
Painted in casein on illustration board in 1960.
From the collection of Mr. and Mrs. W. Eugene McCarron,
Lake Forest, Illinois.

Country Fair Athlete by Camille Bombois.
Painted in oil on canvas, about 1930.
From the National Museum of Modern Art, Paris.

An Artist
Paints a Picture

You can paint a picture
if you have a brush, some paint,
and a piece of paper.
You dip the brush into the paint—
and away you go!
You paint a picture of your mother
or your father or a flower
or a dog—anything.
In a way, you're an artist.
But famous artists had to study
and learn about a lot of things
before they could paint
the kinds of pictures
that you see in this book.
The man you see in this photograph
is a famous Italian artist.
His name is Giorgio de Chirico.
Turn the page
and see how he paints a picture.

The artist decides to paint a picture
of some apples, a pear,
some lemons, and some peaches.
He arranges the fruit on a white cloth.
Then he gets the paints and brushes
that he will need
and puts them on a table,
where he can reach them
while he paints the picture.

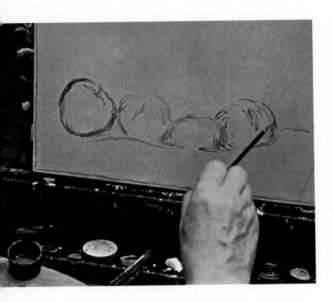

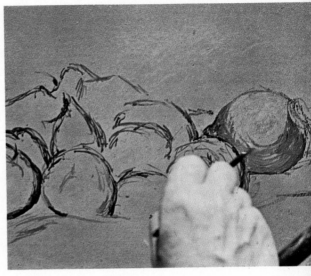

The artist paints the outlines
of the fruit as well as
the outline of the tablecloth.

Then he begins to use colors
to paint in the lemon
and make it look real.

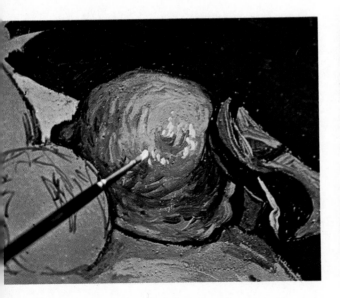

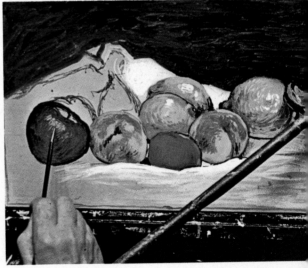

Can you see how his brush marks
make the lemon look as though
you could hold it in your hand?

He is holding a stick
in his left hand
to keep his right hand steady.

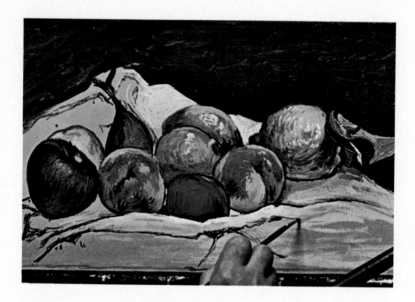

Now, with different colors,
he paints in the other fruit
and part of the tablecloth.

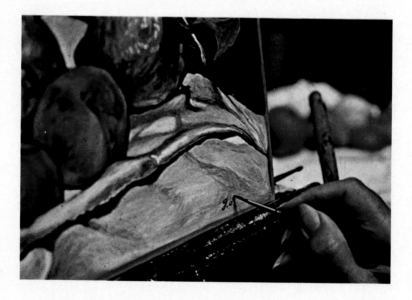

When the picture is finished,
the artist signs his name
in a corner of the painting.

The Family

You are an important part of your family.
So is Mother. So is Father.
So are sisters and brothers,
grandmothers and grandfathers,
aunts and uncles,
and all your cousins.
You might even think of a pet animal
as almost like one of the family.

In the pages that follow,
you will see the way
some artists have looked at families
and put them into paintings and statues.

Maybe you can tell
what this picture is about
just by looking at it.
Pablo Picasso, a Spanish artist,
wanted you to think of this mother
as a symbol of mothers everywhere
who love and protect their children.
So, he painted
a large mother and a large child
and added three things
that the world is made of—
the land, the sea, and the sky.

This painting has a secret.
Turn the page to see what it is.

Mother and Child by Pablo Picasso.
Painted in oil on canvas in 1921.
From The Art Institute of Chicago.

Fragment of *Mother and Child* by Pablo Picasso.
Painted in oil on canvas in 1921.
From The Art Institute of Chicago.

The picture on the opposite page
shows part of a father.
He used to be in the painting
Mother and Child by Pablo Picasso.
The father sat near the mother and child.
Picasso did not like the painting
when it was finished.
Finally,
he decided he would show the mother and child
without the father.
So he cut off a piece of canvas
with part of the father on it.
What happened to the other part?
Picasso painted land, sea, and sky over it.
Look again at the picture
on the opposite page.
Look at the *Mother and Child* on page 21.
Can you see how Picasso changed his work
to make it just what he wanted it to be?

Look at these pages.
A Chinese artist
made the vase a long time ago.
An African artist
carved the statue out of wood.
The vase and the statue
look very different
from each other, don't they?
But something about both
is the same.
Look again.
Can you tell what it is?

Ku Yüeh Hsüan, artist unknown.
Porcelain vase enameled
in the 1700's.
From The Cleveland Museum of Art,
John L. Severance Fund. ▶

Wood sculpture of mother and child,
artist unknown,
◀ from the Luluwa tribe, Kasayi region,
Congo, Africa.
From the Royal Museum
of Central Africa, Tevuren, Belgium.

"When I'm out walking with my father,
I think he's taller than anything —
twice as tall as me,
and much, much taller than my dog,
who's much, much smaller than me."

What is the tallest thing in this picture?
Look again.
It looks as if the artist wants you to think
of the father as the tallest.
But you know
that the far-off hills are much taller.
In what other way has the artist
made the father seem tall?

Joseph Gardner and His Son,
Tempest Tucker
by Jacob Maentel.
Painted in watercolor, about 1815.
From the Abby Aldrich Rockefeller
Folk Art Collection,
Williamsburg, Virginia.

This boy had to sit still long enough
for the artist to paint his picture.
But it wasn't easy.
Doesn't he look as if
he just can't wait to go out and play?

Young Boy by Ernest Crichlow.
Painted in oil in 1960.
From the collection of William B. Branch,
New Rochelle, New York.

Grandma Moses lived through 76 Christmases
before she began to paint pictures.
Then she painted this picture
about all the things that she remembered
about Christmas.
Look—and then look again.
See how many things
you can find in the picture
that help you understand
how Grandma Moses felt about Christmas.

Christmas at Home by Grandma Moses.
Painted in oil on Masonite in 1946.
©Grandma Moses Properties, Inc., New York.

Many Dutch children believe
that St. Nicholas brings
toys, cakes, and candy
to good girls and boys
on the Eve of St. Nicholas, December 5th.
Sometimes, children who have not been
as good as they should receive gifts, too—
gifts they'd rather do without.
Look at the picture.
Do you see the child with the unwanted gift?

The Feast of St. Nicholas by Jan Steen.
Painted in oil on canvas, about 1665.
From the Rijksmuseum, Amsterdam.

Your eyes would probably pop with surprise
if what's happening in this picture
happened at your house.
But you can tell from the way
the artist painted this picture
that this family wasn't one bit surprised.
They thought of the horse
as one of the family.
Notice how casual everybody is.
Look again,
and the picture tells you other things.
You can tell which of the children
liked the horse best.
You can tell whom the horse liked best.
And perhaps you can tell
whom the artist liked best.

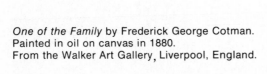

One of the Family by Frederick George Cotman.
Painted in oil on canvas in 1880.
From the Walker Art Gallery, Liverpool, England.

Pierre Auguste Renoir
liked to paint pictures
of pretty women and children.
Renoir painted this picture
of a mother and her daughters
when they were in a park
in Paris, France, almost 100 years ago.

This Mexican mother keeps her baby
with her when she makes tortillas.
A tortilla is a little, round,
flat cake made of dough.
You can see that the mother has to use
both hands to roll the dough.
So, she tucks her baby into the shawl
on her back.
There he sleeps, while his mother works.

Mother and Children
by Pierre Auguste Renoir.
Painted in oil on canvas,
about 1875.
©The Frick Collection,
New York.

Tortillera by Jean Charlot.
Detail from a fresco
painted in the 1900's.
From the University of Georgia
Journalism-Commerce Building,
Athens, Georgia.

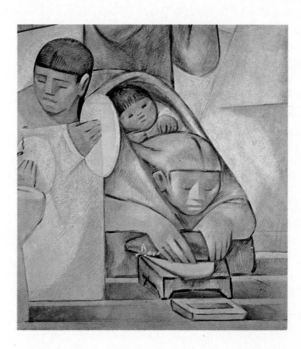

Long ago, a busy ruler lived in Italy.

His name was Ludovico Gonzaga.

Ludovico was such a busy man

that he hardly had time

to pose for a picture

with his family and friends.

He may have kept on working

while the artist painted this picture.

How does the picture tell you this?

Family and Court of Ludovico Gonzaga II
by Andrea Mantegna.
Detail of a fresco painted about 1474.
From the Palazzo Ducale, Mantua, Italy.

Do you think this is a different way
for an artist to do a picture of a family?
Is it a painting?
Look again.
Is it a statue?
Look again.
Can you tell which parts of the picture
are painted
and which parts are carved from wood?

The Family by Marisol (Marisol Escobar).
Construction of painted wood and other materials
done in 1962.
From The Museum of Modern Art, New York,
Advisory Committee Fund.

Do you ever watch people?
Perhaps you look at the people
you see on the street
or in pictures,
and you try to guess
what they do and where they live.

Look at this photo of a family.
Do you think they live in the city
or on a farm?
Who are the oldest?
Who are the youngest?
What else can you guess about them?
And can you guess
whose pictures are on the wall?

Family Portrait.
A photograph by Nina Leen, 1948.
The Museum of Modern Art, New York.

When the sculptor made this statue
he first looked at a real family.
Then he used his imagination
to show the family
in a new and different way.
You know that it is a statue of a family
as soon as you look at the picture.
That's because you look at it,
not just with your eyes,
but also with what you know about families.
What makes the mother and father
seem so strong?
What makes you know
that they protect the child?
What makes you know
that the child depends upon his mother?

Family Group by Henry Moore.
A bronze sculpture cast in 1950.
From The Museum of Modern Art, New York,
A. Conger Goodyear Fund.

People at Work

Firemen and football players
have jobs that are exciting.
But most people have jobs
that may not be exciting
in the same way—
jobs they go to every workday;
jobs in offices and factories,
and other places.
In this section, you can see
how artists have shown
people at work
in many kinds of jobs.

Going to the store can be a chore.
So can walking the dog,
or doing any small job that you do.
Sometimes, you get paid
for doing chores,
but most of the time you don't.
In France, where people like
fresh-baked bread every day,
bringing home a loaf from the bakery
is one of the most common chores.

French Bread by Red Grooms.
An extension painting on wood done in 1963.
From the Harry N. Abrams
Family Collection, New York.

It takes more people
than you may think
to get a letter
to the place it's going—
especially when you send a letter
overseas.

The sailors in this picture
are on a ship
that came from across the sea.
They are lifting bags of mail
from the ship
and passing them
to the men on the tugboat.
The tugboat will carry
the mail to shore.

Can you find the names
of cities or countries
the mail came from?

Transfer of Mail from Liner to Tugboat
by Reginald Marsh.
A fresco painted in 1935.
From the Post Office Department,
Washington, D.C.

*S*ection men strained their backs
shoveling snow from railroad tracks.
Sometimes, they worked night and day
before the train was on its way.
And when the tracks were finally clear,
the train drove off with the engineer.

Now, snowplows clear away the snow —
but engineers still make trains go!

American Railroad Scene: Snow Bound.
Currier and Ives lithograph, 1871.
From the Coverdale and Colpitts Collection, New York.

Fire engines belong in a firehouse.

Butchers sell chickens in chicken markets.

Whoever heard of a butcher

who sells chickens in a firehouse?

Look at the picture.

The butcher

is standing in front of a chicken market.

But look again.

The red building looks like a firehouse.

The artist who painted this picture

must have thought

the idea of selling chickens

in a firehouse was funny.

Do you?

Gallinas Vivas by Robert Sivard.
Painted in oil in 1962.
From Michael Stewart, New York,
courtesy of Midtown Galleries.

These are artists at work—
four sculptors in their studios.

Sculptors make models
of clay or wax,
or weld and shape metals
into unusual forms,
or cast statues in bronze,
or chisel statues
from stone or wood.

Henry Moore
shaping a model.

Giacomo Manzù
making a clay sculpture.

Alexander Calder
cutting metal for a sculpture.

Richard Stankiewicz
welding a metal sculpture.

Some of the best dishes are made of china.
And *porcelain* is the name of
an especially fine kind of china.
Long ago, an artist made this
porcelain statue of another artist at work.

In the statue, both the lady and the artist
are dressed in fine clothes.
So, what could be more fitting
than to use fine china to make the statue?

Look again.
You can see how carefully the artist
is looking at the lady.
It isn't easy to paint a picture
that will please the lady
and almost everyone else who sees it, too.

The Portrait by Anton Grassi.
A porcelain done about 1780.
From the Museum
für Kunsthandwerk,
Frankfurt am Main, Germany.

The Russian women
in this painting
work in a pottery factory.
They are carefully coloring
the designs on pots
and bowls and spoons.
Take a look at the dishes
in your kitchen.
Do you think any of them
could have been
made in this way?

Khokhloma by Margarita Kasyanova.
Painted in oil in 1963.

Sunshine comes softly
through the window
and covers the room
and everything in it
with a golden light.
The sunshine falls
on the milkmaid's white cap,
on her quiet face,
and on her strong bare arms.
Even the chunks of bread
look golden.

The Milk Maid by Jan Vermeer.
Painted in oil on canvas, about 1658.
From the Rijksmuseum, Amsterdam.

Do you ever daydream at school,
when you should be studying?
Sometimes,
grown-ups in offices daydream, too.

Office in a Small City by Edward Hopper.
Painted in oil on canvas in 1953.
From The Metropolitan Museum of Art, New York,
George A. Hearn Fund, 1953.

What do you see first when you look
at this painting of a woman making a hat?
Is it the colors the artist used?
Is it the way the light spreads
through the room and shines on the woman?
Does the woman look interested
in the work she is doing?
Do you get the idea
that the woman is just about to take the pin
out of her mouth and stick it in the hat?
If you see all these things,
you are seeing some of the skills
that made Degas a famous painter.

The Millinery Shop by Edgar Degas.
Painted in oil on canvas, about 1882.
From The Art Institute of Chicago,
Mr. and Mrs. Lewis Coburn Memorial Collection.

This wall painting came from a tomb
built in Egypt more than 3,000 years ago.
It shows people making bricks
of clay and sand from the Nile River,
and water from a nearby pool.
The people put the mixture into molds
that shaped the bricks
that dried in the sun.
The bricks were used to build buildings.

Today, bricks are still used
to build buildings.
So are lots of other materials—
like the steel beams
ironworkers use
to build a skyscraper.

Wall painting from Theban tomb
showing brickmaking,
artist unknown.
Painted in the 1400's B.C.

The Builders by Fernand Léger.
Painted in oil on canvas
in 1950.
From the Musée Fernand Léger,
Biot, France.

Some fishermen fish in deep water at sea.

Others fish along the shore.

Look at the pictures on these pages.

You see some fishermen using nets

to catch many fish at one time.

You see other fishermen using tall spears

to catch a few fish at a time.

Can you tell which fishermen

are fishing in deep water,

and which are fishing along the shore?

Which group seems to be having more fun?

The Herring Net by Winslow Homer.
Painted in oil on canvas in 1885.
From The Art Institute of Chicago,
gift of Mr. and Mrs. Martin A. Ryerson.

Fishermen Drawing Nets by Walter Battiss.
Painted in oil in the 1900's.
From the South African National Gallery, Cape Town.

An artist painted this picture
more than 200 years ago.
It shows that people
have been interested in science
for a long time.
The teacher and others
are gathered around a machine
called an *orrery*.
The machine helps the teacher
show how the earth
and other planets
move around the sun.
Can you tell
what stands for the sun
in this painting?

The Orrery by Joseph Wright.
Painted in oil on canvas, 1763–1765.
Reproduced by permission of
the Derby Museum and Art Gallery,
Derby, England.

Astronaut Gordon Cooper
became the first man to orbit the earth
in two separate space flights —
the first in 1963,
the second two years later.
In this painting, he has returned from space
and, after being picked from the sea,
he walks on the deck of the recovery ship
—taking his first steps
since he went into orbit.

First Steps by Mitchell Jamieson.
Painted in acrylic in 1963 for NASA.
From the National Aeronautics
and Space Administration, Washington, D.C.

Land, Sea, and Sky

You walk or ride across the land
and sail across the sea.
And sometimes, you may fly through the sky
in a plane.

Artists look at land, sea, and sky
and paint pictures of the things they see.
They paint pictures of land and trees
and things that move across the land,
such as trains.
They paint pictures of the seas
and things that move across the seas,
such as ships.
They paint pictures of the sky
and things that move across the sky,
such as planes.
And sometimes, they paint pictures of things
that they imagine, such as men with wings.
Turn the pages, and see pictures of land,
sea, and sky, and of the way people travel.

The land, the sea, and the sky
are filled with movement.
Trees move in the wind.
Waves move in the sea.
And clouds move in the sky.

Olive Grove by Vincent Van Gogh.
Painted in oil on canvas in 1889.
From the Rijksmuseum Kröller-Müller,
Otterlo, The Netherlands.

Wave on Rock by John Marin.
Painted in oil on canvas in 1937.
From the estate of the artist.

Sky Above Clouds III by Georgia O'Keeffe.
Painted in oil on canvas in 1963.
From a private collection.

▼

The artist who painted this picture
filled the land, sea, and sky
with real and make-believe
ways to travel and things to do.
Wouldn't it be fun to live in
the land of *The Magic Mountains*?
You could have a snowball fight
in the morning and a
summertime picnic in the afternoon.
You could paddle a canoe or pole a raft.
You could go ice-skating or swimming.
You could drive a farm tractor
or go sailing in a balloon.
You could visit an elf
in his snug little house
or a mermaid out on her rock.
You could even take a ride
in a flying saucer or on a magic carpet.

The Magic Mountains by Peggy Burrows.
Painted in watercolor and tempera in 1968.
From the Field Enterprises Educational Corp. Collection.

This picture is full of noise.

The engine chugs.

The train wheels squeal.

The waterfalls roar.

Wouldn't it be fun to be on the train,

listening to the sounds

and looking out the train window

at Niagara Falls?

Panoramic View of Niagara Falls
with a Michigan Central Railway Train
by Robert R. Whale.
Painted in oil on canvas in the mid-1800's.
From the collection of
Mr. and Mrs. Jules Loeb,
Lucerne, Quebec, Canada.

La Gare St. Lazare by Claude Monet.
Painted in oil on canvas in 1877.
From The Louvre, Paris.

Rolling Power by Charles Sheeler.
Painted in oil on canvas in 1939. ▶
From Smith College Museum of Art,
Northampton, Massachusetts.

Fewer and fewer steam locomotives
pull trains now.
But not too long ago,
it was just as exciting
to visit a railway station
as it is to visit an airport today.
You could stand alongside the locomotive
and watch the big wheels begin to roll
as the train moved, and steam and smoke
filled the station.

What good is a wagon
that can't carry anything?
It's good for making you wonder
and use your imagination.
Maybe that's what the artist
who made this wagon wanted you to do.

Wagon II by David Smith.
A forged iron sculpture done in 1964.
From the estate of the artist.

Hot desert winds have piled dry sand
against the stone base of the huge Sphinx
near Al Jizah in Egypt.
The hot desert sun beats down on the Sphinx
and the stone pyramids in the distance.
Through the heat and sand of the desert,
a caravan passes.

Pyramids by Oskar Kokoschka.
Painted in oil on canvas in 1929.
From the Nelson Gallery
Atkins Museum (Friends of Art Collection), Kansas City, Missouri.

During the War of 1812,
an American ship and an English ship
fought in a famous battle.
The name of the American ship
was the *Constitution.*
The name of the English ship
was the *Guerrière.*
Long after the war was over,
an artist painted this picture
of what he imagined
the ships looked like during the battle.
Can you tell from the painting
who won the battle?

The Constitution and the Guerrière
by Thomas Chambers.
Painted in oil on canvas, about 1845.
From The Metropolitan Museum of Art, New York,
gift of Edgar William
and Bernice Chrysler Garbisch, 1962.

In Venice, Italy,
canals are used as streets,
and people often ride in boats
to get around the city.
Venice still looks much the same
as it did long ago,
when the artist
painted this picture
of the "main street" —
the Grand Canal.
But one big difference is that,
today, you can see motorboats
on the canal.

The Grand Canal with Rialto Bridge
by Francesco Guardi.
Painted in oil on canvas in the 1700's.
From the Fine Arts Gallery of San Diego,
San Diego, California.

Indians who live in northwestern Canada
use canoes for traveling and fishing.
The canoe is a useful boat.
It can be made to move very fast,
and a canoe that holds four people
is light enough for one man to carry.
But a canoe is not useful when it leaks.
These men are making sure
that their canoe is watertight.
They are putting some sticky stuff
called *resin* on the seam of the canoe.
The fire keeps the resin soft enough
for the men to spread it with the board.

Mending the C.P.R. Canoe
by Thomas Fripp.
Painted in watercolor
in the late 1800's
or early 1900's.
From the McCord Museum,
McGill University,
Montreal.

Ship-building, Gloucester Harbor
by Winslow Homer.
A woodcut made in 1873
for *Harper's Weekly.*
From the Newberry Library,
Chicago.

If you had lived in New England
a hundred years ago,
as these boys did,
men building a sailing ship
would be an everyday sight.
The boys
are more interested in building
their own wooden boats
to sail in ponds and pools.

The boat glides down the Missouri River
with hardly a sound.
The boy looks at the smooth water,
and he smiles.
Even the pet fox looks quiet
and comfortable in the warm, misty air.
But look at the fur trader
in his stocking cap.
Why do you think he looks so grumpy?

Fur Traders Descending the Missouri
by George Caleb Bingham.
Painted in oil on canvas, about 1845.
From The Metropolitan Museum of Art, New York,
Morris K. Jesup Fund, 1933.

The ocean and boats in this painting
don't look the way they would
in a photo.
But as soon as you look at the painting,
you know that it is a picture of boats
moving on the waters.
Can you name the different kinds of boats
in the picture?

The Motor Boat by Lyonel Feininger.
Painted in oil on canvas in 1931.
From The Cleveland Museum of Art,
gift of Julia, wife of Lyonel Feininger.

Some men have dreamed of flying
with wings on their backs.
But have you ever dreamed of flying
on a butterfly or a bumblebee,
or by umbrella, the way Mary Poppins did
in books and a movie?
You can travel any way you want to
in a dream,
just as the people are doing
in these paintings.

Flying Men by Francisco Goya.
An aquatint and etching, 1810–1819.
From The Metropolitan Museum of Art, New York,
Harris Brisbane Dick Fund, 1924.

Le Jour se Lève Piétons Celestes Descendez
by Gertrude O'Brady.
Painted in oil on canvas in 1939.
From Mr. and Mrs. John W. McBrady, Chicago.

Leonardo da Vinci designed a parachute
more than 400 years ago.
Scientists worked for many years
to improve Da Vinci's design and make it work.
Finally, a French scientist used a parachute
to make a successful jump from a tower.
There weren't any airplanes in those days,
and the scientist wanted to show
how people could use parachutes
to jump from high buildings in case of fire.
Now skydivers, like the one in the painting,
use parachutes to land safely on earth
after jumping from highflying planes.

Sketch of parachute
done about 1495
by Leonardo da Vinci.
Reproduced from
Il Codice Atlantico
in the collection of
IBM Corporation.

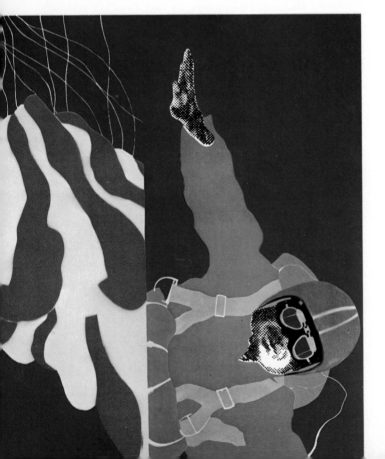

Skydiver 3
by Gerald Laing.
Painted in oil
on canvas in 1964.
From the Harry N. Abrams
Family Collection, New York.

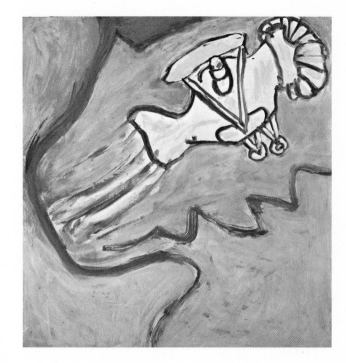

Ascending Icarus
by Hugh Weiss.
Painted in oil
on Masonite in 1964.
From the collection
of Jacques Massol, Paris.

Photograph by James B. Johnson.
▼

Everyone admired
Charles Lindbergh's bravery
when he flew
across the Atlantic Ocean
in a single-engine plane,
something like the one
in the painting above.
Now, people fly
across the ocean every day
and nobody's surprised,
not even
when they see fighter planes,
such as those in the photo,
roar across the sky at more
than 1,000 miles an hour.

At first glance,

the bicycle and its rider

seem to be standing still.

But look again,

and you will see some things

that show you that the young man

and the bicycle are moving.

For example, look at the foxtail

at the end of the long, thin pole.

What else do you see

that tells you

the bicycle is moving?

Young America by Andrew Wyeth.
Painted in egg tempera on a gesso panel in 1950.
From The Pennsylvania Academy of the Fine Arts,
Philadelphia.

Shoes can have round toes

or pointed toes or square toes or open toes,

but shoes never have ten toes—

except in this painting.

The Red Model
by René Magritte.
Painted in oil on canvas in 1937.
©Nationalmuseum, Stockholm.

Outdoors

Outdoors is a special place to be.
It's where the sun shines,
night falls,
and day breaks.

Outdoors is where you can see
buildings and bridges,
streets and strangers,
farms and factories,
and things that take you places.

Outdoors is where you can see
exciting, colorful things,
if you take a good look at what's around you.
That's what artists do
when they make pictures
of what they see in cities,
in villages, and in the countryside.

An artist painted this picture
of a city like Siena, Italy,
more than 600 years ago.
Many of the buildings look different
from those that you see in cities today.
People are wearing different clothes
from those we wear now.
And no cars or buses fill the streets.
But even so, you can see that
cities have always been big, busy places
where many people work, live, and play.

The Effects of Good Government on the City
by Ambrogio Lorenzetti.
Detail from a fresco done about 1338.
From the Palazzo Pubblico, Siena, Italy.

Some city streets are clean and quiet.
Other streets,
like the one in this painting,
are messy, crowded, and noisy.
If you painted a picture of a city street,
how would you paint it?

The City by Xavier González.
Painted in oil, 1954–1955.
From the collection of the artist.

These three pictures
have something in common.
You can tell
what the weather is like
in each scene.
It's not hard to tell,
for instance,
that the man and woman
with the umbrellas
are walking in the rain.
What kind of weather
do the other pictures show?

Place de l'Europe on a Rainy Day
by Gustave Caillebotte.
Painted in oil on canvas in 1877.
From The Art Institute of Chicago,
Charles H. and
Mary F. S. Worcester Fund.

▲

Une Baignade, Asnieres
by Georges Seurat.
Painted in oil on canvas,
1883–1884.
From The National Gallery, London.

Backyards, Greenwich Village
by John Sloan.
Painted in oil on canvas in 1914.
Collection Whitney Museum
of American Art, New York.

▼

In streets and parks and palace gardens,
fountains of every shape and size—
fancy or funny—
are joyful things to look at,
touch,
and listen to.
Fountains spout silvery streams of water
that splash and spray
and, on sunny days, catch the light
and make a thousand rainbows.

Il Mascherone
by Pirro Ligorio.
A limestone sculpture
done in 1550.
Villa d'Este,
near Tivoli, Italy.

Storks at Play
by Augustus Saint-Gaudens and
Frederick MacMonnies.
A bronze sculpture
done in 1887.
Lincoln Park, Chicago.

Fountain of the Northwest
by James Fitzgerald.
A bronze sculpture
done in 1962. Grand Courtyard
of Seattle Center's Playhouse,
Seattle, Washington.

Trains travel on tracks
on city streets, under city streets,
and even above city streets.
The trains that run overhead are *elevated.*
People call the elevated train, the *el.*
The trains that run under the ground
are *subway* trains.
Sometimes, the *el* travels above the street,
and then goes down under the ground.
Can you imagine what it's like
to be the motorman who drives the train?

Chicago by Red Grooms.
Construction done in 1967.
From the Allan Frumkin Gallery, Inc., Chicago.

The Brooklyn Bridge crosses the East River
in New York City.
The bridge has two towers, one at each end.
The bridge hangs from steel ropes
that are attached to the towers.
The artist who painted this picture
looked through the archways of the tower
at one end of the bridge.
Do you see the other tower and the cables?
What else do you see?

The Brooklyn Bridge: Variation on an Old Theme
by Joseph Stella.
Painted in oil on canvas in 1939.
Collection Whitney Museum of American Art, New York.

Chartres Cathedral by Camille Corot.
Painted in oil on canvas in 1830.
From The Louvre, Paris.

Gelmeroda IX
by Lyonel Feininger.
Painted in oil on canvas in 1926.
From Museum Folkwang, Essen, Germany. ▶

Look at these two paintings of churches.
You can see the same shapes in both of them.
You can see steeples that point to the sky
and windows that curve at the top.
You can see three-sided shapes
and you can see four-sided shapes.
But see how differently each artist
has put the shapes together
to make different paintings of churches.

After a farmer harvests his crops,
he may take some to market,
and he may store some in his barn
and in his *silos*
so that he can feed his animals
all year round.
Look at the farm painting.
The silos are the tall round buildings
that look like towers.
The buildings in the other painting
are a part of the Ford automobile factory
in River Rouge, Michigan.
The tall concrete tubes all in a row
are used to store coal.
The coal is burned in the furnaces
to make the heat that is used to shape
the steel that becomes part of the cars.
In what way are the tall concrete tubes
like silos?

September Harvest
by John Wheat.
Painted in oil and tempera on Masonite in 1953.
From a private collection.

Classic Landscape by Charles Sheeler.
Painted in oil on canvas in 1931.
From the collection of Mrs. Edsel B. Ford,
Grosse Pointe Shores, Michigan.

This picture shows how Indians lived
in North America about 400 years ago.
It is an engraving by Theodore DeBry
made from a painting by John White.
The letters explain the parts of the picture.
"A" is the building that held the graves
of the Indian chiefs.
"B" is where the Indians met to pray.
"C" is where they met on special days.
"D" is where they had parties.
"E" is where they grew tobacco.
"F" is where an Indian sat
and scared away the birds and beasts
who came to eat the corn that grew
in "G" and "H", the fields for growing corn.
"I" is where pumpkins grew.
"K" is where the Indians built fires
on feast days.
"L" is the river where they got water.

Village of Secotan
by Theodore DeBry (after John White).
Copperplate engraving, 1590–1602.
From The Thomas Gilcrease Institute, Tulsa, Oklahoma.

TB   20

This windmill was painted
by a Dutch artist named Jacob van Ruisdael.
He enjoyed painting outdoor scenes
of the Netherlands—
a land where windmills
are an everyday sight.
If Ruisdael lived in your town today,
what do you think he would enjoy painting?

Mill near Wijk bij Duurstede
by Jacob van Ruisdael.
Painted in oil on canvas, about 1670.
From the Rijksmuseum, Amsterdam.

Everything in this painting
is standing still—
yet you get the feeling of rolling.
Look at the hills
that you could roll down!
Look at the roads
that bikes and cars could roll along!
And can you imagine
the things you could do
on the rolling hills in winter?

Stone City, Iowa by Grant Wood
Painted in oil on wood in 1930.
From the Joslyn Art Museum, Omaha, Nebraska.

A rich lord once lived
in this French castle.
From the castle towers,
he could watch his people
working in the field.
He could see far across the field.
If an enemy approached the castle,
the lord had time to warn his people.
Then the people would hurry into the castle,
pull up the bridge,
and fight the enemy from behind the walls.

The painting
and the numbers and words above it
are all part of a 500-year-old calendar,
called the *Book of Hours.*
This part is for July.

July, from the Duc de Berry's *Book of Hours*
by the Limbourg Brothers.
Illuminated manuscript, about 1410.
From the Musée Condé, Chantilly, France.

Winter's ice crackles and drips
in the soft spring air of a hilly forest.
The drips plunk into pools
that gurgle over rocks,
then splash into streams
that race into roaring rivers.

Deep in a tropical forest,
where wild flowers bloom,
monkeys chatter and birds sing.

The Coming of Spring
by Charles E. Burchfield.
Painted in watercolor on paper, 1917–1943.
From The Metropolitan Museum of Art, New York,
George A. Hearn Fund, 1943.

The Jungle: Monkeys and Oranges
by Henri Rousseau.   ▶
Painted in oil on canvas in 1908.
From a private collection.

Buildings and cars look as small as toys
when you see them from an airplane
flying high in the sky.
And you can see the shapes
of forests, fields, and rivers.
Sometimes, miles of earth seem to be made
of squares, wavy lines, and ribbons of color.
Do these photos of date gardens and fields
and hilly farmlands remind you
of some of the paintings in this book?
Which ones?

Animal Fair

Animals can be large or small,
as round as a ball or as skinny as a stick.
An animal can be soft and furry,
like a kitten,
or hard and prickly, like a porcupine.
An animal can be swift and graceful,
like a gazelle,
or slow and clumsy, like a tortoise.
Animals can crawl, creep, slither, or slide.
They can run, jump, climb, swim, or fly.
They can be friendly.
They can be frightening.

Most of all, animals are interesting.
That's one reason artists
make pictures and statues of them.
After you look at the animals
in this section,
perhaps you can try to paint
a picture of your pet.

Elephants, ostriches, lions, and hogs,
Monkeys and rabbits and zebras and dogs,
Birds and giraffes and camels and bears.
Thousands of animals went in by pairs—
In through the window
And in through the door,
Until Noah's Ark couldn't hold any more.
Each kind of beast and each kind of bird—
Can you imagine the noise Noah heard?

Noah's Ark by Joseph H. Hidley.
Painted in oil on wood, about 1865–1872.
From the Abby Aldrich Rockefeller
Folk Art Collection,
Williamsburg, Virginia.

This cat and its master, Julie Manet,
belonged to a well-known family.
Julie's mother was Berthe Morisot,
a famous French painter.
Julie's uncle was Édouard Manet,
another famous French painter.
And the man who painted this picture
of Julie and her cat
was Pierre Auguste Renoir,
still another famous French painter.

Julie Manet with Cat by Pierre Auguste Renoir.
Painted in oil on canvas in 1887.
From a private collection, Paris.

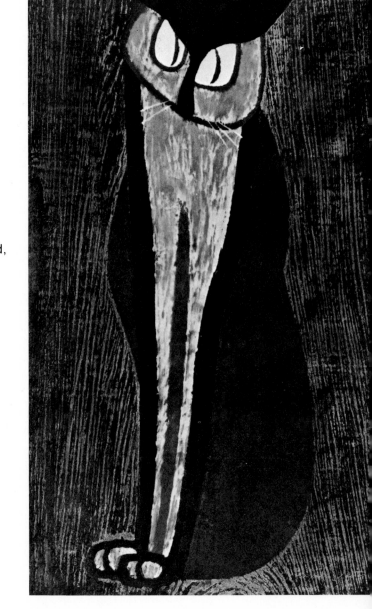

Did you ever see a cat
that looks like this cat?
Its head is shaped
like a Siamese cat's head.
But it has too much white
on its face
to be a Siamese cat.
It isn't an Angora cat
because its head isn't pointed,
and its fur isn't long.
It's not a Tabby
because it has no stripes.
It can't be a Calico
because it has no spots.
But it doesn't matter
that it's not
Siamese or Angora
or Calico or Tabby.
It's a "Look Again" cat—
from Japan!

Steady Gaze by Kiyosho Saito.
A wood block print done in 1948.
From The Art Institute of Chicago.

Poor little gray mouse!
It's afraid of cats.
It's afraid of owls.
It's always watchful.
Maybe it'll have time
to pick a berry,
then scamper away
before a cat or an owl comes by.

The Chinese letters on the picture say:
"How could you call this stealing if it
doesn't mind being caught in the act?"
The Chinese letters also say: "Painted
by Ch'i Pai-Shih at age 90."

Mouse, Painted in Washes of Black and Gray
by Ch'i Pai-Shih. An ink wash done in the mid-1900's.
Formerly owned by Alice Boney.

*T*hump-thump-thump
goes the dog's leg
while it scratches its ear,
where a flea is hiding.

Bow-wow!

A hare looks like a rabbit,
but it's bigger and stronger,
and its ears are much longer.
It hides all day
and looks for food at night.

The hare in this picture
looks so quiet
it's hard to believe
that hares ever act strangely.
But, in the month of March,
hares hop and twist and jerk
all over the place.

As a matter of fact,
when we want to describe
a person who acts
in an odd way, we may say,
"He's as mad as a March hare."

Young Hare by Albrecht Dürer.
Painted in watercolor in 1502.
From Fonds Albertina, Vienna.

Monkeys play
most of the day.
But the time comes,
when even monkeys like to rest.
And what could be nicer
on a summer day
than to sit or lie
on the soft green grass?

The Chinese writing
on this picture
tells when it was painted
and who painted it.

Monkeys by Mori Sosen.
Brush painting
in ink on paper, Kyoto School, about 1800.
From the Museum of Fine Arts, Boston,
Bigelow Collection.

David Twining had a farm,
Ee-eye, ee-eye, oh!
And on this farm
he had some turkeys,
Ee-eye, ee-eye, oh!
With a gobble, gobble here,
and a gobble, gobble there —
here a gobble,
there a gobble,
everywhere a gobble, gobble.
David Twining had a farm,
Ee-eye, ee-eye, oh!

What sounds would you hear
from the other animals
you see in this picture
of David Twining's farm?

The Residence of David Twining, 1787
by Edward Hicks.
Painted in oil on canvas, 1845–1848.
From the Abby Aldrich Rockefeller
Folk Art Collection,
Williamsburg, Virginia.

Only two of the five cows
in this painting
seem to know
that you are watching.
They turn their heads
to look at you.
The other cows
pay no attention.
One continues to eat grass.
Another has settled down
to rest.
And the white cow
stands over a pail
while she's being milked.

Have you ever milked a cow?

Farm at Laeken by Peter Paul Rubens.
Painted in oil on wood, 1617–1618.
By permission of
Her Majesty the Queen,
Buckingham Palace, London.
Copyright Reserved.

What a fuss in the barnyard!
Cluck, cluck, cluck, clucks the hen.
Cheep, cheep, cheep, peep the chicks.
Gobble, gobble, gobble, goes the turkey.
Cock-a-doodle-do, crows the rooster.
Each animal makes a different sound.
They all live together
in the barnyard.
That is their home.

The Barnyard
by Melchior di Hondecoeter.
Painted in oil on canvas in the mid-1600's.
From The Detroit Institute of Arts, Detroit,
gift of Mr. and Mrs. Edgar B. Whitcomb.

Mother ducks pick feathers
from their chests
to line their nests.
The feathers are called *down*.
People like to stuff pillows
with down because it is so fluffy.
You can see how the artist
has painted the feathers.
What other soft and fluffy things
do they make you think of?

Ducks by Alexander Max Koester.
Painted in oil on canvas
in the late 1800's or early 1900's.
From the Charles and Emma Frye
Art Museum, Seattle.

An American woman artist
carved these little lambs
out of hard rock,
called *granite.*
But the artist
had the skill
to make the lambs
look soft and warm,
even though the stone
from which the lambs were carved
is hard and cold.

Twin Lambs by Sylvia Shaw Judson.
A granite sculpture done in 1947.
From the collection of the artist,
Lake Forest, Illinois.

White sheep, black sheep
have lost their way.
They might as well stay
where they are
until someone finds them.

An English artist painted
everything in the picture
to look as real as possible.
Do you think this picture
looks more like a painting
or looks more like a photo?

Strayed Sheep by William Holman Hunt.
Painted in oil on canvas in 1852.
From The Tate Gallery, London.

Watch the foal
taking milk from the mare.
Smell the fresh grass.
Feel the breeze warmed by the sun.
Listen to the birds in the trees.
It's spring.

Mares and Foals by George Stubbs.
Painted in oil on canvas, about 1760.
From the collection of the Duke of Grafton.
Reproduced by permission
of Soho Gallery, London.

This horse is a bronco.
It's wild
and it wants to stay free.
It fights to throw the cowboy to the ground.
But the cowboy wants to tame the bronco.
He knows that he must stay in the saddle,
or the horse will not be tamed.

Frederic Remington,
the artist who made this statue,
knew how broncos act.
He was a cowboy as well as an artist.

The Bronco Buster
by Frederic Remington.
A bronze sculpture
done in 1909.
From the Philbrook Art Center,
Tulsa, Oklahoma.

This is a war horse.
It has been trained to obey
every command—even in battle.
Its rider,
Bartolommeo Colleoni,
was a general who lived in Italy
more than five hundred years ago.

Equestrian monument
of General Bartolommeo Colleoni
by Andrea del Verrocchio.
A bronze sculpture
done in the late 1400's.
St. John and
St. Paul Square, Venice.

It's not easy to get close to wild deer.
Make the tiniest sound,
and they leap out of sight.
Deers don't go looking for fights.
But all male deer and some female deer
have weapons to protect themselves.
Their weapons are their antlers.

Study of two stags' heads and one doe's head
by Pisanello (Antonio Pisano).
Drawn in pen on white paper in the early 1400's.
From the Cabinet des Dessins, The Louvre, Paris.

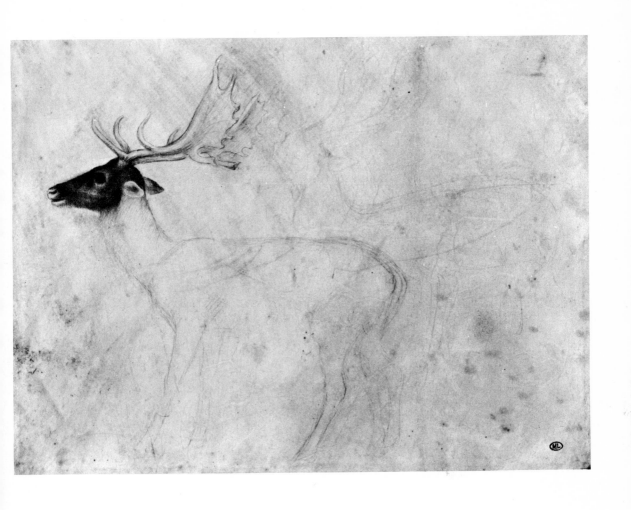

Study of two stags
by Pisanello (Antonio Pisano).
Drawn in silverpoint and watercolor
on parchment in the early 1400's.
From the Cabinet des Dessins, The Louvre, Paris.

A fire spreads
across the prairies of Canada.
The ground trembles,
as the hoofs of frightened buffalo
make a sound like thunder
that grows louder and louder,
until the air seems to fill
with the wild noise.
Prairie chickens and other animals
fly away from the fire
and from the crushing hoofs
of the rushing buffalo.

The Buffalo Stampede
by Frederick A. Verner.
Painted in oil in 1882.
From the Ernest E. Poole Foundation,
Edmonton, Canada.

Run for your life!
The prairie is burning!
The wind whips the flames so high
that the sky seems to be on fire.
Indians on horseback ride faster and faster
away from the fire.
The antelopes follow, leaping and running.
And the wolves move swiftly and silently
through the dry prairie grass.

The artist who painted this picture
is a Kiowa-Comanche Indian,
named F. Blackbear Bosin.

Prairie Fire by F. Blackbear Bosin.
Painted in watercolor in 1953.
From the Philbrook Art Center, Tulsa, Oklahoma.

These hunters, on horseback and on foot,
carry sharp spears and curved swords.
They attack the lions.
The lions roar and fight back.
The hunters must fight
with all their might
to kill the lions,
or the lions will kill them.

The Lion Hunt by Eugène Delacroix
Painted in oil on canvas in 1861.
From The Art Institute of Chicago,
Potter Palmer Collection.

A Persian artist painted this picture
of how soldiers fought long ago.
Drums beat.
A trumpet blasted.
Arrows shot through the air.
The battle was on!

The Persian words on the painting
tell how the elephant
helped win the battle.

*Battle between Khusraw Terviz Troops
and Bahram Tchoubine* by Hayder Kouli.
Painted in pigment on parchment in the early 1600's.
From the Bibliothèque Nationale, Paris.

It looks like a big,
old, tired cat
resting in the sun.
But look out!
It's no ordinary cat.
It's a tiger!

Tigre Royal by Eugène Delacroix.
A lithograph done in 1829.
From The New York Public Library—
Astor, Lenox and Tilden Foundations.

Artists can use almost anything
to make a statue.
They can use clay or wood
or metal or stone.
Or they can use ivory,
which comes from tusks.
Tusks are the long pointed teeth
of elephants, walruses,
and some other animals.

Here, you can see
a goose made of ivory
from elephant tusk,
a hunting scene made of ivory
from walrus tusk,
and a whale made of bronze.

Do you think the statues would be
rough or smooth to your touch?

Polar Bears, Eskimo, and Walrus
carved in ivory, artist unknown.
From the California
Academy of Sciences,
San Francisco, Liebes Collection.

An ivory toilet dish
in the form of a trussed bird,
done about 1350 B.C.
From The Brooklyn Museum,
New York.

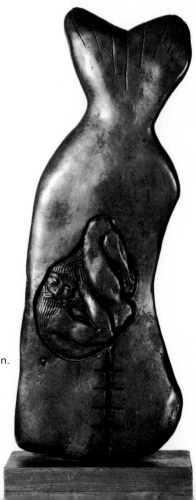

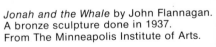
Jonah and the Whale by John Flannagan.
A bronze sculpture done in 1937.
From The Minneapolis Institute of Arts.

A rhinoceros is enormous
and scary-looking.
But, unless you bother it,
it is quiet and harmless.
So, you can see
that things sometimes look
a lot different
from what they are.

As you can see in the picture,
the metal statue of a rhinoceros
is really a desk.
How would you like to own a desk
that looks like a scary animal?

Rhinoceros by François-Xavier Lalanne.
Made of brass and steel in 1966.
From a private collection, New York.

Someone once decided
to name this statue *Ram in the Thicket.*
But, as you can see, the animal is a goat.

A billy goat has long, messy whiskers,
and it doesn't smell good.
A billy goat goes around saying "Maaaa"
and chewing up almost everything in sight.

But long ago, some people believed
that a billy goat was a holy animal.
One of these people was the artist
who made this statue.

Ram in the Thicket, artist unknown.
A sculpture in gold, silver, and shell
done about 2700 B.C.
From the University Museum
of the University of Pennsylvania, Philadelphia.

Bearded Bull's Head,
artist unknown.
A cast copper sculpture
of the period 2800 to 2600 B.C.
From the City Art Museum
of St. Louis.

Elephant by Anne Arnold.
A wood sculpture done in 1963.
◄ From the collection of
Mr. and Mrs. Howard Wise,
New York.

Galactic Insect by César
(César Baldaccini).
A welded iron sculpture
done in 1956.
From The Museum of Modern Art,
New York, gift of
G. David Thompson.

Clay and stone and wood and bone
and even paper and cloth
are some of the *materials*
an artist can use
to make a statue.
But an artist always
chooses the material
that he thinks will fit
the kind of statue
he wants to make.
The artist who made the statue
of a big bug
chose scraps from a pile of junk.
You can see that the bug
looks rough and scratchy.
How do you think the statues
of the elephant and the bull
would feel to you
if you could touch them?

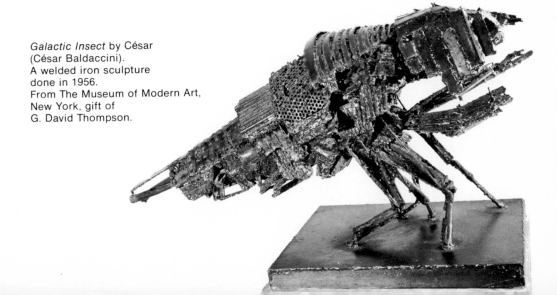

Lots of people eat fish —
big fish, little fish, scaly fish, snaky fish,
and some fish that don't even look like fish.

In ancient Italy, an artist made this *mosaic*
with tiny bits of colored stone.
The mosaic shows some of the kinds of fish
that some people eat.
Which ones would you like to eat?

Roman Menu, artist unknown.
Detail from a mosaic of the 1st century B.C.
From the Museo Archeologico Nazionale, Naples.

There never were,
and never will be,
such odd-looking fish
in such a strange-looking sea.

And the little man
in the funny hat—
do you think he'd be safe
in a boat like that?

The Seafarer by Paul Klee.
Painted in watercolor in 1923.
From the collection of T. Dürst-Haass,
Muttenz, Switzerland.

These pictures show
two different ways
that artists have made statues of birds.
One statue looks like a real pigeon,
except that you can take it apart
and fill it with candy.
Move the cranes around,
and they can be face to face,
or back to back.
Which do you like better—
the pigeon or the cranes?

Tureen with cover: in form of Pigeon, artist unknown.
A tin enameled faïence (soft earthenware)
done in the mid-1700's.
From The Metropolitan Museum of Art, New York,
gift of R. Thornton Wilson, 1950,
in memory of Florence Ellsworth Wilson.

Cranes and Serpents, artist unknown.
Lacquered wood sculpture of the period
481–221 B.C.
From The Cleveland Museum of Art, J. H. Wade Fund.

Once, there was an artist
who liked birds so much
that, instead of going to work,
he used to go looking for birds
in the countryside.
Then he'd paint pictures of them.
For a while, he lived in Louisiana,
where he probably painted
this picture of a heron.
The artist became famous for the way
he made the birds in his pictures
look just as they do in real life.
His name was John J. Audubon.
Do you think this bird looks real?

Louisiana Heron by John James Audubon.
Painted in watercolor in 1832.
From The New-York Historical Society.

If you look carefully at this picture,
you can see more
than birds on a branch.
You can see the artist's name.
It looks like a small flower
in the lower left-hand corner
of the picture.
And you can see the marks, or seals,
of the people who have owned this picture
from the time it was painted
more than seven hundred years ago.
The seals are the marks
you see along the edges of the painting.
There's one catch, though.
To read the artist's name
and the owners' seals,
you have to know how to read Chinese.
The artist's name is Ma Lin.

Birds on a Branch
by Ma Lin.
Painted on silk
in the early 1200's.
From the Museum
of Fine Arts, Boston,
Ross Collection.

A plover is a small bird.
But when a bunch of plover fly together,
they look like a fast-moving cloud.
You can almost hear their wings beating
when you look at this painting.
Take another look—and listen.
And if you've ever heard
the sound of plover,
maybe you'll even hear them calling.

Flight of Plover by Morris Graves.
Painted in oil on composition board in 1955.
Collection Whitney Museum of American Art, New York,
gift of Mr. and Mrs. Roy R. Neuberger.

This vulture is sometimes called a buzzard.
Sometimes, it's called a turkey buzzard.
But whatever it's called,
look how long its wings are!
Look how smoothly it flies!
You can almost imagine
you're flying, too—
up, up, up,
soaring in circles.

Soaring by Andrew Wyeth.
Painted in tempera on Masonite in 1950.
From the Webb Gallery of American Art,
Shelburne Museum, Shelburne, Vermont.

Horse-drawn carriages
like the one in this painting
once crowded the streets of Nassau,
the capital of the Bahamas.
Now, most people ride in automobiles
or on bicycles.
Only a few horse-drawn carriages remain
to remind people of the old days,
and to take tourists around the city
to see the sights.

Horse and Buggy by Ludwig Bemelmans.
Painted in mixed media in the early 1950's.
From the Field Enterprises Educational Corp. Collection.

This tapestry, a picture on cloth
woven with colored wool or silk threads,
could cover a good-sized bedroom floor.
But it wasn't used as a rug.
It decorated a wall inside a French castle
more than 400 years ago.
The tapestry seemed to bring
a garden with animals indoors.
The tapestry is one of a set of six
known as *The Lady with the Unicorn.*
The unicorn is
the only make-believe animal in it.
Do you know which one it is?

The Lady with the Unicorn, artist unknown,
from the Atelier Loire.
One of a set of six tapestries, 1509–1513.
From the Cluny Museum, Paris.

An old story about Saint George
and the dragon
tells how Saint George
saved a beautiful princess
from being swallowed by a wicked dragon.
Just in time,
Saint George rode up on his white horse
and killed the dragon.

This picture tells a part of the story.
You can see the princess,
dressed in her crown and royal robes.
You can see Saint George
aiming his spear at the dragon.
What do you think happened next?
Well, the spear broke.
And Saint George had to
pull out his magic sword
and kill the dragon.
Can you see the magic sword?

St. George and the Dragon by Bernardo Martorell.
Painted in tempera on a panel, about 1438.
From The Art Institute of Chicago.

Before people knew how to write,
they painted pictures
to tell about
the animals they saw.

How many animals
in the picture
can you see at the zoo?

The Small Mufflons, artists unknown.
Mural of the period 5000 to 4000 B.C.
At Sefar in Tassili-n-Ajjer, Algerian Sahara.
Document Mission Henri Lhote.

Imagine This!

When you look into a fun-house mirror,
you see yourself
in a way you have never imagined.
And when you look at the paintings
and statues in this section,
you'll see how artists
can use their imaginations
to show things in other ways
you have never imagined.

Your face is a shape with other shapes in it.
Your eyes have more than one shape in them,
and so does your nose and your mouth.
Look at the pictures.
One artist painted a picture of a man's head
by using different kinds of fruits
and vegetables for shapes.
The other artist made a statue of a head
by putting together circles,
squares, and triangles.
Look in a mirror.
How many different shapes do you see
in your face?

Head # 2 by Naum Gabo.
A painted galvanized iron
sculpture done in 1916.
From the collection
of Miriam Gabo,
Middlebury, Connecticut.

The Gardener by Giuseppe Arcimboldo.
Painted in oil on wood, about 1590.
From the Skokloster Castle and Collection, Sweden.

Are all monsters scary things,
ready to grab you or gobble you up?
Maybe not.
The giant head with its mouth open
is a picture of a temple
shaped like a monster.
In fact, the picture is inside
a real temple in Thailand.
And, in the smaller painting,
the one-eyed monster
was one of many giant shepherds,
known as Cyclops,
that the people of Greece
once believed lived under volcanoes.

Detail of fresco depicting part
of the story of Ramakien.
Artist unknown.
Painted in the early 1800's.
From Shrine of the Emerald
Buddha, Bangkok, Thailand.

*The Deformed Polyp Floats on
the Strand, a Kind of Smiling
and Hideous Cyclops,* Plate III
from *Les Origines* by Odilon
Redon. A lithograph done in
1883. From The Museum of
Modern Art, New York,
gift of Victor S. Riesenfeld.

A man with imagination began to build
some towers in his yard.
He kept building the towers for years,
using thousands of sacks of cement,
and thousands of seashells,
pop bottles, broken dishes,
and chunks of tile.
He grew old while building the towers.
When he finished them, he gave them away.
Then he moved from his home in Watts,
a part of Los Angeles.
The man's name was Simon Rodia,
and his towers are now famous.

Did you ever take bits and pieces
of paper or cloth
and paste them on a cardboard
to make a picture?
If you did, you made a *collage*.
What did the artist use
to make the collage you see in this picture?

Collage by Kurt Schwitters.
A paper collage done about 1934.
From The University of Arizona Museum of Art, Tucson,
The Gallagher Memorial Collection.

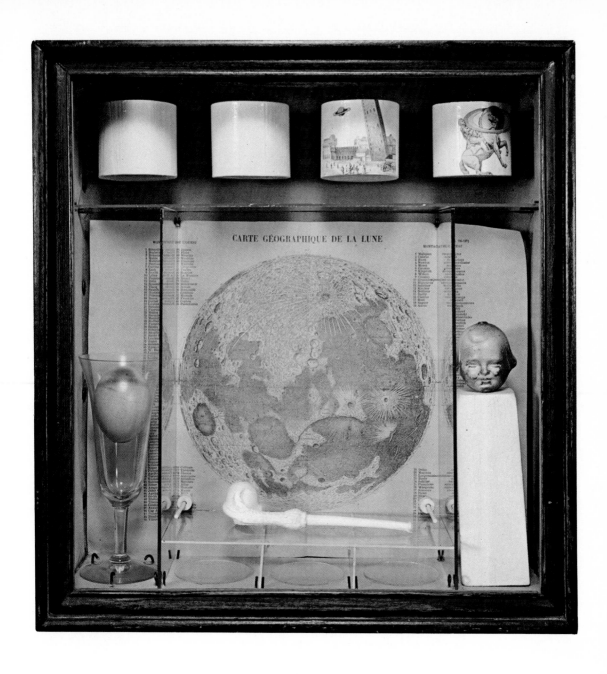

Soap Bubble Set
by Joseph Cornell.
Construction done in 1936.
From the Wadsworth Atheneum,
Hartford, Connecticut.

Can you imagine
making a picture in a box?
That's what this artist did.
He collected the objects that you see,
and put them together
to make a picture in a box.
It might be fun to see
how you would make a picture in a box.

The tea set is just for show.
It's covered with fur from head to toe.
And you couldn't eat the loaf of bread
with 42 raisins as big as your head.

You wouldn't drink from a fur-lined tea set
or eat bread made of canvas.
But you can look at these things
that two different artists made
and maybe laugh with them.

Did you ever see such a funny cup?
It's lined with fur from the saucer up.
Did you ever see such a funny bread?
It's longer than your parents' bed.

Object by Meret Oppenheim.
◀ Fur-covered tea cup, saucer, and spoon done in 1936.
From The Museum of Modern Art, New York.

Raisin Bread: 5 Slices and End, 42 Raisins
by Claes Oldenburg.
Canvas, glue, Liquitex, and wood sculpture done in 1966.
From the collection of Mr. and Mrs. Joseph Helman,
St. Louis.
▼

Everything in this painting is possible,
except one thing.
Clouds float in the sky.
Waves roll on the sea.
And some castles are built on rocks.
What is the one impossible thing
that the artist did, perhaps to surprise you
and make you wonder
and look and look again?

The Castle of the Pyrenees
by René Magritte.
Painted in oil on canvas in 1959.
From the collection of Harry Torczyner, New York.

You remember
that Humpty Dumpty
broke into pieces
when he fell off the wall.
Well, this is how an artist
put Humpty Dumpty together again.
How would you
put the pieces
of Humpty Dumpty together?

Humpty Dumpty by Isamu Noguchi.
A ribbon slate sculpture done in 1946.
Collection Whitney Museum
of American Art, New York.

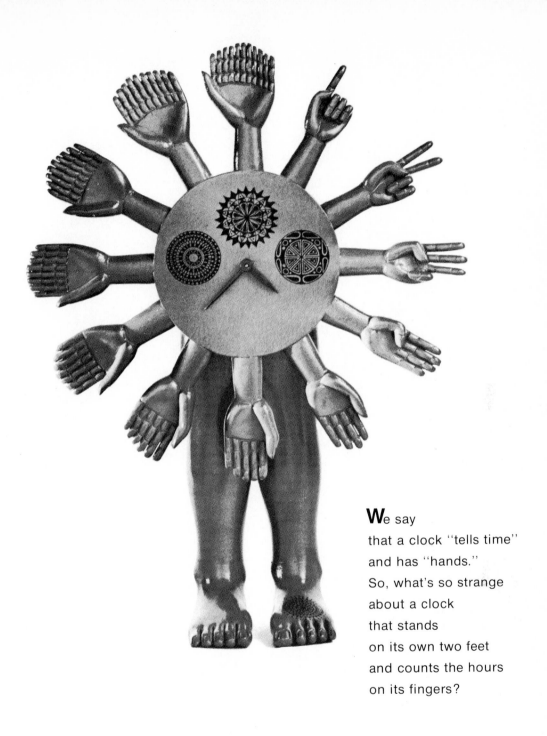

We say
that a clock "tells time"
and has "hands."
So, what's so strange
about a clock
that stands
on its own two feet
and counts the hours
on its fingers?

"Hand" Clock with Two Legs
by Pedro Friedeberg.
Carved and painted wood, 1964.
From the Byron Gallery, New York.

Books and bottles, apples and lemons,
and tables and trays are everyday things.
But artists have painted pictures of them
in many unusual ways.
Do you see anything the artist has done
to make this painting different from
other paintings of tables and books
and bottles and fruit?

Still Life: The Table
by Georges Braque.
Painted in oil on canvas in 1928.
From the National Gallery of Art, Washington, D.C.,
Chester Dale Collection.

These pages and the two pages that follow
show you paintings made of squares,
spots and splashes of color,
and lines that dip, swirl, and curve.
You can enjoy just looking at the colors
and letting your eyes follow the lines.
Or you can look again
and use your imagination.
What do you see?

Kauai #2
by Charles W. Bracken.
Painted in watercolor in 1968.
From the Field Enterprises Educational Corp. Collection.

Sketch I for Composition VII
by Wassily Kandinsky.
Painted in oil on canvas in 1913.
From the collection of Felix Klee, Bern, Switzerland.

*Large Composition with Red,
Blue, Yellow* by Piet Mondrian.
Painted in oil on canvas in 1928.
From the Sidney Janis Gallery,
New York.

Cathedral
by Jackson Pollock.
Mixed media on canvas, 1947.
From the Dallas Museum of Fine Arts,
Dallas, Texas,
gift of Mr. and Mrs. Bernard J. Reis.

▶

Bank of Ambiguities
by Jean Dubuffet.
Painted in oil on canvas in 1963.
From the Museum of Decorative Arts,
Paris.

▼

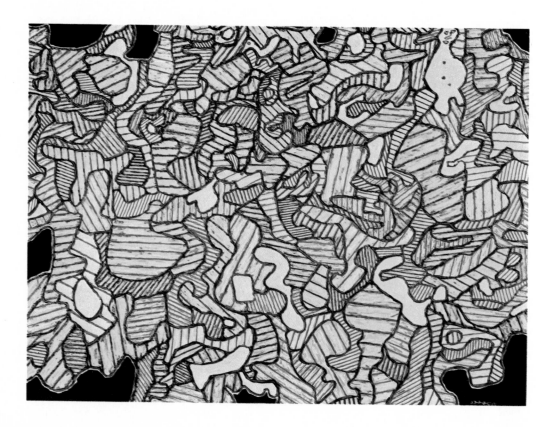

An artist imagined what it was like
at the end of a famous battle
fought more than 2,000 years ago.
He painted this picture
with so many soldiers and horses
that it is almost impossible to count them.
The words at the top of the picture
are in Latin, and they say:
"Alexander the Great finally defeats Darius
after having killed about 100,000
foot soldiers and 10,000 horsemen,
and having captured Darius' mother, wife,
and children, who were fleeing in disorder
with 10,000 horsemen."
And that's what the picture is about.
Alexander the Great was king of Macedonia,
and Darius was king of Persia.

The Battle of Alexander
by Albrecht Altdorfer.
Painted on wood in 1529.
From the Alte Pinakothek, Munich, Germany.

Here's a painting that seems to move!
First, you see one thing,
and then you see another.
How many squares do you see?
Look again.
You may have missed a few.
Can you guess what makes the lines
seem to move?

Square of Three—Yellow and Black
by Reginald H. Neal.
Lithographed on canvas in 1964.
From The New Jersey State Museum,
Trenton, New Jersey.

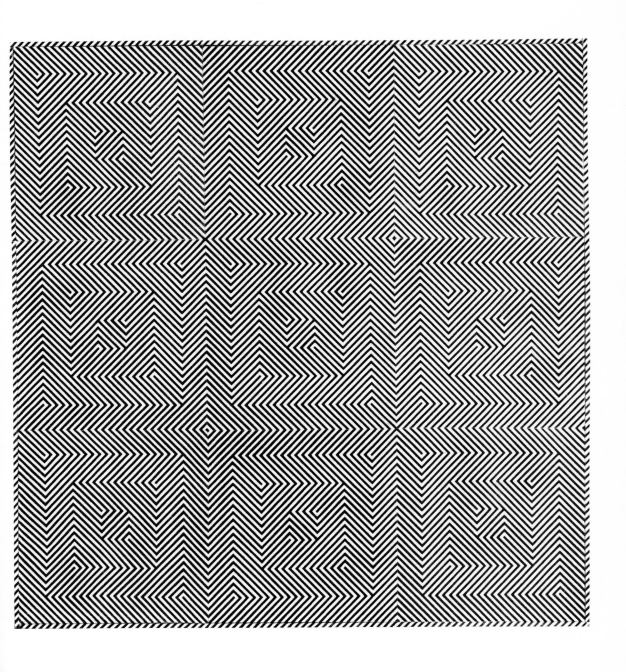

Fun and Games

Let's go to a ballgame;
let's see a play.
How about a horse race, or the ballet?
Let's play the piano;
let's sail the sea;
let's play checkers, you and me!

This section shows pictures and statues
of people enjoying fun and games.

Posters are colorful signs,
often with pictures
that quickly tell you
what's happening, and where.
Which of these posters
excites you the most?

Peintures Murales by Joan Miró.
A silk-screen poster done in 1961.
From Poster Originals, Ltd., New York.

Silk-screen poster done in 1967
by Roy Lichtenstein.
From Poster Originals, Ltd., New York.

Poster by Alphonse Mucha
advertising a play
at Theatre de la Renaissance, Paris.
A color lithograph done in 1898.
From the Victoria & Albert Museum,
London,
and by special permission
of Jiri Mucha.

Bruant aux Ambassadeurs
by Henri de Toulouse-Lautrec.
Lithographic poster done about 1892.
From the collection of
Mr. and Mrs. Michael Hoffner,
Park Ridge, Illinois.

Poster for Columbian Exposition 1893.

One of a series of posters
by University of Mexico students,
for the 1968 Olympic Games.

Silk-screen poster done in 1968
by William J. Lloyd.
From the Container
Corporation of America, Chicago.

Children play leapfrog and roll-a-hoop,
pick-up-jacks and piggyback.
They did 400 years ago, too,
when the artist painted this picture.
How many other games
that you know how to play
can you find in the painting?

Children's Games
by Pieter Breughel the Elder.
Painted in oil on oakwood panel in 1560.
From the Kunsthistorisches Museum, Vienna.

Children sometimes have playthings
that artists make especially for them,
such as stone horses
in a city playground.
And sometimes, children make playthings
from any odds and ends they can find.
The Japanese children in the painting
are using rocks and stones they have found
to build a kind of tower called a *stupa.*

The Japanese words in the painting
give the title of the picture
and the artist's name.

Sculptural horses
by Constantino Nivola.
Cast concrete sculpture
done in 1964.
New York City
Housing Authority
playground, New York.

*Children Piling Stones
to Make a Stupa*
by Tomioka Tessai.
Painted in ink
and watercolor on a silk
scroll in 1917.
From Kiyoshi-Kōjin
Seicho Temple,
Takarazuka, Japan.

What can you do on a rainy day at home?
You might play the piano.
You might play checkers.
Or you might play cat's cradle.
All you need for that
are your own two hands
and a piece of string.

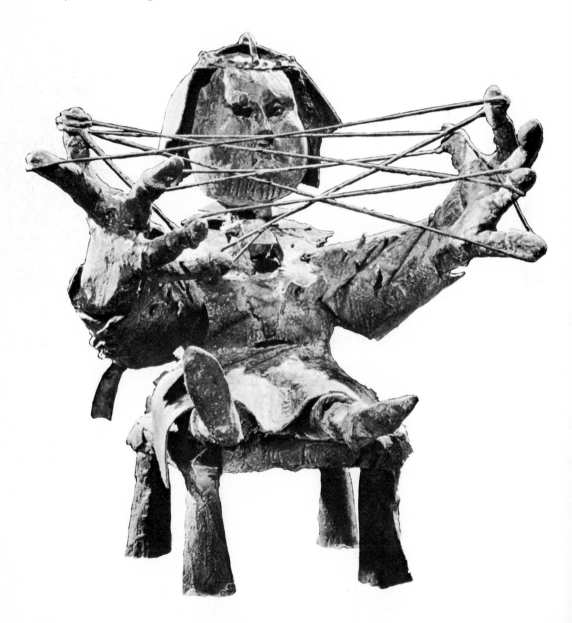

Checker Game and Piano Music
by Henri Matisse.
Painted in oil on canvas in 1923.
From a private collection.

Seated Dwarf with Cats Cradle
by Bernard Reder.
◀ A bronze sculpture cast in 1960.
From the collection of
Mrs. Bernard Reder, Tel Aviv-Yafo.

When people dance, they move their bodies,
their arms, and their legs in time to music.
And when artists watch people dancing,
they can see the different lines and shapes
in each movement that a dancing person makes.
In the painting from Poto-Poto,
in French Congo, Africa,
the artist painted the waving arms
and pounding feet of the dancers
by using long, skinny lines.
Francis Picabia, the artist
who painted the picture on the other page,
used triangles, circles, and squares of color
to show how people move when they dance.

Musicians with Three Drums by Ondongo.
Painted in watercolor in 1960.
From the Africa Collection of Rolf Italiaander,
Hamburg, West Germany.

Dances at the Spring by Francis Picabia.
Painted in oil on canvas in 1912.
From the Philadelphia Museum of Art,
Louise and Walter Arensberg Collection.

Edgar Degas liked to go to the theater
and watch *ballerinas* dance and move about.
He always carried a sketch book
and made quick drawings of the dancers.
Then he went home and carefully drew,
painted, or made statues of ballerinas.
The action that Degas saw
in a split second,
people can see every time
they look at Degas' paintings and statues.

Rehearsal of the Ballet on the Stage by Edgar Degas.
Painted in oil on paper mounted on canvas, about 1874.
From The Metropolitan Museum of Art, New York,
the H. O. Havemeyer Collection.

Ballet Dancer, Dressed by Edgar Degas.
◀ A bronze sculpture cast by A. A. Hebrard in 1921
from the wax figure done by Degas in 1880.
From the Henry P. McIlhenny Collection, Philadelphia.

Fast music, slow music,
loud music, soft music —
dance to it, march to it,
listen to it,
watch musicians play it.
Look at the painting on the next page
of the man with the saxophone.
What kind of music do you think
he is playing?
What kind of music do you think
the men are playing in the other painting?

Song of the Towers by Aaron Douglas.
Painted in oil in 1966.
From Executive Residence,
Madison, Wisconsin, gift of Links, Inc.

String Quartette by Jack Levine.
◄ Painted in tempera and oil, 1934–1937.
From The Metropolitan Museum of Art, New York,
Arthur H. Hearn Fund, 1942.

What is Ruby Green singing—
a lullaby or a love song?
It doesn't matter.
The important thing is
that the artist shows you a young girl
with bright, shining eyes and a soft smile
who sings a song that makes her happy
and gives you pleasure just to look at her.

Ruby Green Singing by James Chapin.
Painted in oil on canvas in 1928.
From the Norton Gallery and School of Art,
West Palm Beach, Florida.

Central Park — Winter
by William James Glackens.
Painted in oil on canvas
in the late 1800's or early 1900's.
From the Metropolitan
Museum of Art, New York,
George A. Hearn Fund, 1921.

The Boating Party by Mary Cassatt.
Painted in oil on canvas, 1893–1894.
From the National Gallery of Art,
Washington, D.C.,
Chester Dale Collection.

Whether it's summer or winter,
a day at the park can be fun.

Basketball, wrestling,
and other sporting events
are exciting to watch
and exciting to take part in.
That's why sports have always been
a favorite topic for artists.
An American painter used splashes of color
to show the thrilling start
of a basketball game.
A Greek sculptor made his statue
of wrestlers look as real as possible.
The next time you watch a sporting event,
think how it might look to you
if you were an artist.

Basketball
by Elaine de Kooning.
Painted in tempera
on gesso cardboard in 1960.
From the Graham Gallery,
New York.

The Wrestlers
by unknown Greek sculptor, School of Lysippos.
Marble sculpture done about 300 B.C.
From the Uffizi, Florence, Italy.

"There goes the ball, back, back, *back*—
over the fence for a home run!"
Little League or Big League,
a baseball game means excitement and fun
to the players and the fans who watch.
The artist who made this *construction*
captured some of the fun of the game
by making it a game that you can play with
if you get tired of just looking at it.
You lay it flat and spin the bats.
The ball bounces and shows you your play.
It's just like baseball—
three strikes and you're out.

Baseball Machine by Leo Jensen.
A painted polychrome wood sculpture done in 1963.
From the collection of the artist.

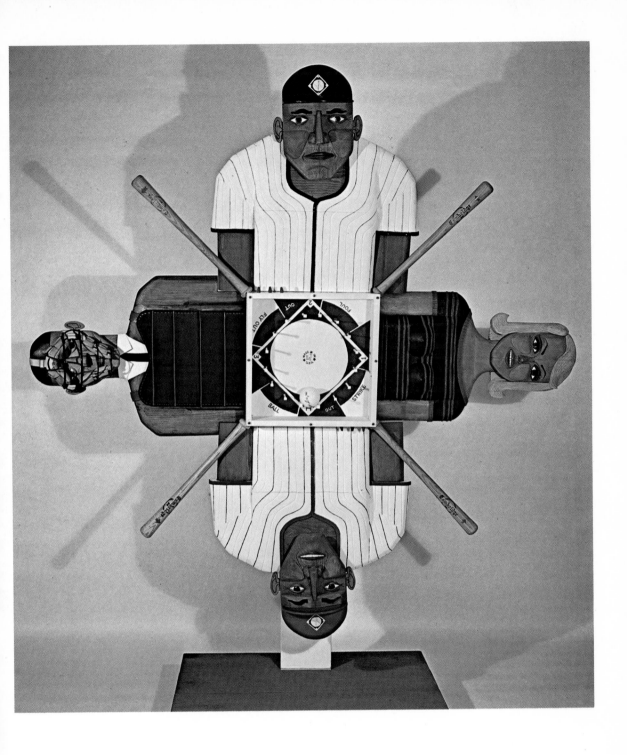

Today, boxers must wear gloves
when they fight in the ring.
But more than 100 years ago,
when this picture was painted,
boxers fought each other
with bare knuckles.
What else do you see
in this painting
that is different
from the way
modern prize fights look?

Bare Knuckles by George A. Hayes.
Painted in oil on cardboard, about 1860.
From the collection of
Edgar William and Bernice Chrysler Garbisch.

Passing Leap
by John Steuart Curry.
Painted in oil on gesso board
in 1932.
From Abbott Laboratories,
North Chicago, Illinois.

The Trapeze Artists
by Fernand Léger.
A colored lithograph done in 1950, ▶
from his portfolio, *Cirque.*
From The Art Institute of Chicago

John Steuart Curry, an American artist,
and Fernand Léger, a French artist,
painted these pictures of trapeze artists.
When you look at Curry's painting,
at the top of the facing page,
you feel almost as though you were
at the circus, watching the performance.
The other painting shows how Leger imagined
the way trapeze artists
feel while performing.

A three-ring circus has come to town,
with elephants and clowns.
What else do you see at a circus?

Circus Elephants by John Marin.
Painted in watercolor in 1941.
From The Art Institute of Chicago,
The Alfred Stieglitz Collection and Robert A. Waller Fund.

Cirque Medrano
by Henri de Toulouse-Lautrec.
◀ Painted in oil and wash
on cardboard mounted on paper in 1893.
From the collection of C.D. McCormick, Chicago.

People

Billions of people live in the world.
But each and every one is different.
And although people are alike in many ways,
there's only one person like you—
and that's you.
When an artist paints a picture
or carves a statue of a person,
he tries to show what makes that person
different from anyone else,
not only in the way he looks,
but in the way he thinks and acts.
Look at the faces of people you see—
your family and friends.
Look again!
Think about how
you would paint their pictures
or carve their statues.

Head by Amedeo Modigliani.
A limestone sculpture
done about 1912.
From the Solomon R. Guggenheim Museum,
New York.

Head of Mayan Man, artist unknown.
A stucco sculpture
of the period A.D. 500 to 900.
From the National Museum of
Anthropology, Maya Room, Mexico City.

Bust of George Bernard Shaw
by Sir Jacob Epstein.
A bronze sculpture done in 1934.
From the City Museum and Art Gallery,
Birmingham, England.

Brass head from Wunmonije Compound,
Ife, Nigeria, artist unknown.
Of the period A.D. 900 to 1300.
From the Museum of Ife Antiquities,
Ife, Nigeria.

Whether nearby or in faraway places,
people are people, and faces are faces.

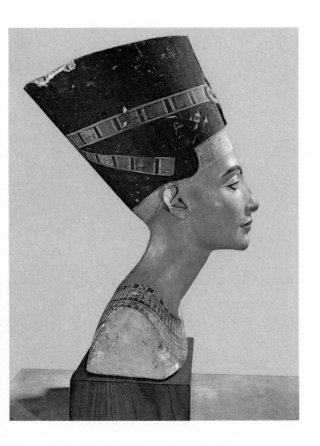

Bust of Queen Nefertiti, artist unknown.
A limestone sculpture done about 1355 B.C.
From the Staatliche Museen,
Egyptian Section, Berlin.

Bust of Madame de Serilly
by Jean Antoine Houdon.
A marble sculpture done in 1782.
From The Wallace Collection, London.

Japanese actors sometimes wear funny masks
to make the audience laugh
between acts of a serious play.
These masks are called *Kyogen* masks.
The actor who wears the mask in this picture
plays the part of Kobuaku,
a funny, angry man.

Kobuaku, artist unknown.
Painted wood Kyogen mask
of the period 1600 through 1700's.
From the Tokyo National Museum.

A *Banda* mask is a kind of religious mask
worn by some members of the Baga tribe of
Guinea on the west coast of Africa.
This mask combines human features
with parts of the crocodile and the antelope.

Banda Mask, artist unknown.
Made of wood, bone, and hair
in the 1800's or 1900's.
From the Bernese Historical Museum,
Bern, Switzerland.

▶

Hundreds of years ago,
artists in what is now Mexico
were not allowed to use turquoise on a mask—
unless it was a mask of a king or a god.
This is a mask of the god of fire.

Mosaic mask, artist unknown.
Wood decorated with turquoise,
colored shells, and corals, Mixtec-Puebla style.
From the Museo Preistorico Etnografico
Luigi Pigorini, Rome.

The Blue Clown
by Walt Kuhn.
Painted in oil on canvas in 1931.
Collection Whitney Museum of American Art, New York.

Clowns and actors paint their faces
to change their looks.
If you wanted to paint a smile on your face,
would you make the corners of your mouth
go up or down?

The actor Bando Hikosaburo III
as he appeared in the drama *Sugawara no Michizane*.
Japanese print by Katsukawa Shunyei.
Done in the late 1700's or early 1800's.
From The Metropolitan Museum of Art, New York,
bequest of Henry L. Phillips, 1940.

Wouldn't you like to
have your picture painted
by one of the most famous artists
of all time?
The young lady in this picture did —
about 500 years ago in Florence, Italy.
She had four sisters and two brothers.
One of her brothers may have introduced her
to the young artist who painted her picture.
The painting has become
one of the most prized paintings of all —
not because of the girl,
but because of the way
the artist painted her.
And because of the painting,
some people still remember the girl's name
— Ginevra de'Benci.
And because of this and other paintings,
millions of people remember the artist's name
— Leonardo da Vinci.

Ginevra de'Benci by Leonardo da Vinci.
Painted in oil on a panel, about 1480.
From the National Gallery of Art, Washington, D.C.,
Ailsa Mellon Bruce Fund.

Some famous artists
have a certain way, or *style,* of painting.
When you learn
what an artist's style is like,
you can recognize his paintings
without seeing his signature.
An easy way to begin looking for
Modigliani's style
is to look for faces shaped like eggs
and necks shaped like posts.

Young Girl with Brown Hair by Amedeo Modigliani. ▶
Painted in oil on canvas in 1918.
From a private collection.

Picasso has many different styles.
You can see how his style
differs from Modigliani's style
in the pictures on the opposite page.
And if you look back a page,
you can see how Da Vinci's
style differs from both
Modigliani's and Picasso's styles.

Woman with Scarf by Pablo Picasso. ▶
Painted in oil on plywood in 1953.
From a private collection.

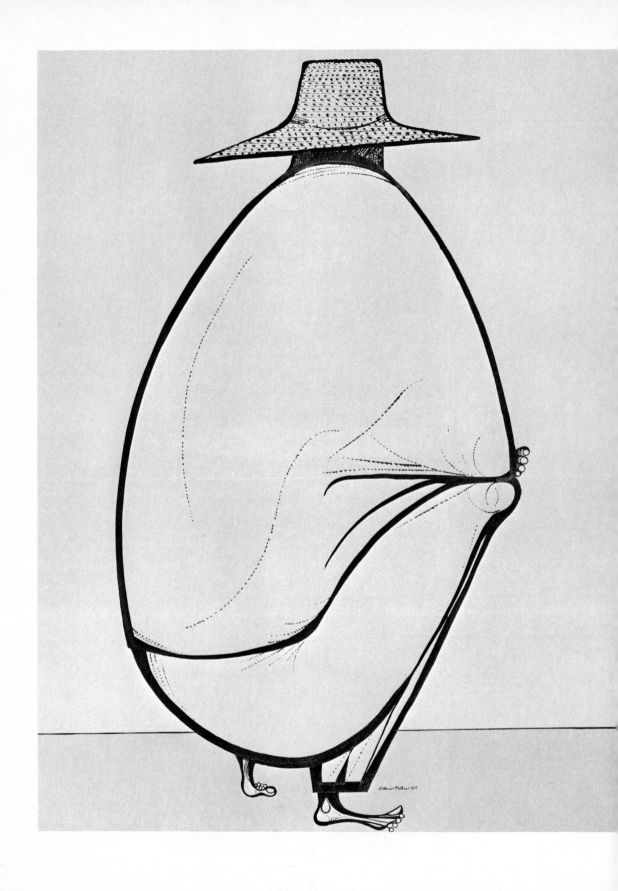

The *Man of Ceara* is so fat
that he looks like an egg wearing a hat.
But in *City Square,* as you can see,
the people are as skinny as they can be.

Man of Ceara by Aldemir Martins.
Drawn in ink in 1945.
From The University of Arizona
Museum of Art, Tucson,
The Edward Joseph Gallagher III
Memorial Collection.

City Square by Alberto Giacometti.
A bronze sculpture done in 1949.
From a private collection.

This little girl is pretending
she is a mother.
The doll is her child
that she dresses, feeds, and loves.

Little girls everywhere enjoy dolls
because dolls are make-believe people
that are fun to play with.

The Little Madonna by George Luks.
Painted in oil on canvas, about 1907.
From the Addison Gallery of American Art,
Phillips Academy, Andover, Massachusetts.

Artists imagine angels and Cupid
as people with wings.
You can see paintings and statues of angels
in museums and in churches.
Many valentines have pictures of Cupid,
and you may have seen statues of Cupid
in gardens and in buildings.

Flying Angel, from the workshop of Jörg Zürn.
Carved in wood in the late 1500's or early 1600's.
From the Los Angeles County Museum of Art,
The William Randolph Hearst Collection.

Two Winged Cherubim by Desiderio da Settignano.
A marble sculpture done in the 1400's.
From the Los Angeles County Museum of Art,
The William Randolph Hearst Collection.

Two famous artists worked together
on this painting
of the Three Wise Men
and others who came to see
the Christ Child
and His mother, Mary.
Look carefully at the expressions
on the faces of the people
around the Mother and Child.
You will see how people felt
about the first Christmas.
The artists put the peacock
into the picture
because, in Christian art,
the peacock means life everlasting.

The Adoration of the Magi
by Fra Angelico and Fra Filippo Lippi.
Painted in tempera
with oil glazes on wood, about 1445.
From the National Gallery of Art,
Washington, D.C.,
Samuel H. Kress Collection.

Thousands of years ago,
Egyptians believed their kings were gods.
And artists made huge statues
such as these look-alike statues
of King Ramses II,
with look-alike statues of his queen
at his feet.
These statues guard a temple at Abu Simbel.
The statues and the temple were carved
in the side of a mountain
close to the Nile River.
They were moved to higher ground
to save them from the waters of a lake
that was formed when the Aswan Dam was built
in the mid-1960's.
In the photo,
you can see people coming out of the temple.
How tall would you guess the statues are?

Great Temple of Ramses II with four huge statues
carved in a mountainside at Abu Simbel, Egypt,
in the 1200's B.C.

V.I.P. stands for *very important person.*
And the people in these paintings
were V.I.P.'s.
One of them was a prince, one was a queen,
one was a king,
and one was an Indian chief.
Which artist would you have chosen
to paint your portrait?

Giuliano de' Medici by Sandro Botticelli.
Painted in tempera with oil glazes on wood, about 1478.
From the National Gallery of Art, Washington, D.C.,
Samuel H. Kress Collection.

Elizabeth I, artist unknown.
Painted in oil on wood, about 1575.
From the National Portrait Gallery,
London.

Syacust Ukah, Cherokee Chief
by Sir Joshua Reynolds.
Painted in oil on canvas in 1762.
From the Thomas Gilcrease Institute,
Tulsa, Oklahoma.

Napoleon by Baron Gérard.
Painted in oil on canvas
in the late 1700's or early 1800's.
From the Southampton Art Gallery,
Southampton, England.

Three different artists—
a photographer, a painter, and a sculptor—
made three different portraits
of President John Fitzgerald Kennedy.
And each of the three artists
tried to catch the expression
that he believed would show people
the kind of man President Kennedy was.

John F. Kennedy. Photograph © by Yousuf Karsh.

President John F. Kennedy
by James Whitney Fosburgh.
Painted in oil on canvas
in 1964.
From the collection of
Jacqueline Kennedy Onassis.

John F. Kennedy, 1917–1963.
Robert Berks, sculptor;
Arnold Newman, photographer.
A bronze sculpture
cast from a clay original
in 1963.
From Garden of Patriots,
Cape Coral, Florida.

This rabbi is a symbol of the Jewish people,
painted by Marc Chagall,
an artist born in Vitebsk,
a city about 300 miles from Moscow, Russia.
The prayer shawl on the rabbi's shoulders
is called a *tallit.*
On his forehead and left arm,
he wears leather straps,
attached to small boxes called *tefillin.*
The boxes contain readings from the Bible.

The Praying Jew (also called *The Rabbi of Vitebsk*)
by Marc Chagall.
Painted in oil on canvas in 1914.
From The Art Institute of Chicago.

Saint Jerome, his hands on the Bible,
was a Roman Catholic priest and scholar,
who translated the Old Testament
from Hebrew to Latin.
A Spanish artist, El Greco,
painted this picture
more than a thousand years
after Jerome died.

St. Jerome by El Greco.
Painted in oil on canvas, probably 1590–1600.
©The Frick Collection, New York.

An artist paints a self-portrait
to show how he sees himself.
Paul Cézanne painted this picture of himself
when he was thirty-seven years old.
A few years later, his friend Renoir painted
the picture of Cézanne on the other page.
Do you think Renoir saw Cézanne
the way Cézanne saw himself?

Self-Portrait by Paul Cézanne.
Painted in oil on canvas in 1875–1876.
From The Louvre, Paris, Laroche Collection.

Portrait of Cézanne
by Pierre Auguste Renoir.
Painted in pastel on paper in 1880.
From the Ittleson Collection, New York.

You have only one face,
but you can change the look on your face
any time you want to.
You can look serious or silly.
You can wrinkle your forehead,
or puff out your cheeks.
You can laugh or cry.

How many different kinds of looks
do you see on the faces in the pictures?

Carl Sandburg. Connecticut. 1936. Montage.
Photograph by Edward Steichen.
From The Museum of Modern Art, New York.

Head of a boy, artist unknown.
A bronze sculpture done in the 200's B.C.
From the Archaeological Museum, Florence, Italy.

Detail from *Portrait of the Jester Calabazas*
by Diego Velázquez.
Painted in oil on canvas, about 1632.
From The Cleveland Museum of Art,
Purchase, Leonard C. Hanna Jr. Bequest.

Tlingit war helmet from southeastern Alaska.
Carved in wood, probably in the 1800's.
From The American Museum of
Natural History, New York,
C. T. Emmons Collection.

Pablo Picasso, the famous artist,
designed this statue
and gave it to the city of Chicago.
As you walk around the big, steel statue,
you might have trouble deciding
what it looks like.
Look at the three views of the statue.
From one side, the statue looks,
to some people,
like the head of a woman.
What do you think it looks like?

You can see more of Picasso's art
on the next two pages.

Chicago Picasso
by Pablo Picasso.
A steel sculpture
done in 1966.
Chicago Civic Center Plaza.

Wherever you see a work of art,
you can look—
and look again.

Various sculptures
by Pablo Picasso
from an exhibition
at the Petit-Palais,
Paris, December 1966.

Books to Read

For Young Readers

Agle, Nan H. and Bacon, Frances E. *The Ingenious John Banvard.* Seabury, 1966. The story of a man who became famous after painting a picture three miles long.

Borten, Helen. *A Picture Has a Special Look.* Abelard, 1961. An explanation of materials used for painting, and some ideas about how to use them.

Glubok, Shirley. *The Art of Ancient Greece.* Atheneum, 1963. An introduction to Grecian art, and how people in ancient Greece lived.
The Art of Lands in the Bible. The art objects that belonged to the ancient people of the Bible are presented in photographs with brief explanations.
The Art of the Eskimo. Harper, 1964. Eskimo art also provides an introduction to Eskimo life.
The Art of the North American Indian. The writer presents the North American Indian, his art and life.
The Art of Africa. 1965. An introduction to African art and African tribal life.
The Art of Ancient Rome. An introduction to Roman art; describes everything from mosaics to monuments that show how people lived in ancient Rome.
The Art of Ancient Peru. 1966. Through Peruvian art, the writer introduces children to how people lived in ancient Peru.

Janson, Horst and Dora. *The Story of Painting for Young People.* Abrams, 1962. A selection of art masterpieces with information about the artists' lives and work.

MacAgy, Douglas and Elizabeth. *Going for a Walk With a Line.* Doubleday, 1959. A guided tour of pictures from Rousseau to Klee by the director of the Dallas Museum of Contemporary Art, and his wife.

Wolff, Robert J. *Feeling Blue.* Scribner, 1968. Picture story about a primary color. *Seeing Red.* Another picture story about a primary color.

For Older Children

Barr, Beryll. *Wonders, Warriors, and Beasts Abounding.* Doubleday, 1967. Artists of various cultures paint pictures of the sky, animals, and soldiers.

Chase, Alice E. *Famous Paintings: An Introduction to Art for Young People.* Platt, 1951, 1962. Art through the ages.
Looking At Art. Crowell, 1966. A book designed to stimulate art appreciation.

Downer, Marion. *Discovering Design.* Lothrop, 1947. The artist uses nature to explain design.

Glubok, Shirley. *Art and Archaeology.* Harper, 1966. An introduction to the subject with photographs of sites in the United States and Europe.

Grigson, Geoffrey and Jane. *More Shapes and Stories.* Vanguard, 1967. Pen, pencil drawings, oils, woodcuts, tapestries, and watercolors form this collection in which the authors write about the content of their selection.

Hunt, Kari and Carlson, Bernice. *Masks and Mask Makers.* Abingdon, 1961. Stories about old and new masks, and how to make some of them.

Kainz, Luise C. and Riley, Olive L. *Understanding Art: People, Things, and Ideas.* Abrams, 1966. An introduction to art appreciation.

Price, Christine. *Made in the Middle Ages.* Dutton, 1961. The history of medieval arts and crafts.
The Story of Moslem Art. 1964. The architecture, painting, and crafts of the Moslem-occupied territories from Spain to India.

Ripley, Elizabeth. *Leonardo da Vinci.* Walck, 1952. The life of Leonardo da Vinci, Italian artist.
Vincent Van Gogh. 1954. The life of the Dutch painter Vincent Van Gogh.
Rembrandt. 1955. The life of the Dutch artist Rembrandt Harmenszoon van Rijn.
Picasso: A Biography. Lippincott, 1959. The life of Pablo Picasso, Spanish artist.
Winslow Homer. 1963. The life of Winslow Homer, American painter.
Velázquez. 1965. The life of Diego Velázquez, Spanish painter.

Rogers, William G. *A Picture Is a Picture: A Look at Modern Painting.* Harcourt, 1964. The development of modern art from Cézanne through the present.

Ruskin, Ariane. *The Pantheon Story of Art for Young People.* Pantheon, 1964. More than 150 illustrations of works of art from the caveman to modern man.

Williams, Jay and Lowry, B. *Leonardo da Vinci.* American Heritage, 1965. A study of the famous Italian painter, engineer, inventor, and scientist, illustrated with his paintings and many sketches from his notebooks.

Illustration Acknowledgments

The publishers of *Childcraft* gratefully acknowledge the following photographers, publishers, agencies, and corporations for illustrations in this volume. Other acknowledgments may be found with each reproduction.

1: Robert Keyes
4: Phoebe Dunn, DPI
6-9: Herb and Dorothy McLaughlin
10: *Childcraft* photo
12-17: Mario De Biasi, Pictorial Parade
18: Phoebe Dunn, DPI
22: *Childcraft* photo by Richard Nickel
29: Vernall Coleman
30: The Galerie St. Étienne, New York City, © Grandma Moses Properties, Inc., New York City
34: © The Frick Collection, New York City
35: *Childcraft* photo by Rem Studios
36: *Childcraft* photo by Giorgio Calzolari
39: Nina Leen, *Life* © Time Inc.
42: *Childcraft* photo
46-47: Robert Crandall
48-49: Thomas Morton
51: *Horizon* magazine
52: *(top)* courtesy of Henry Moore; *(bottom)* *Childcraft* photo by Erich Lessing, Magnum
53: *(top)* photo, John Lewis Stage, Holiday © the Curtis Publishing Company; *(bottom)* *Childcraft* photo by Robert Crandall
54: Alexander Carroux
55: *Soviet Life* magazine
62-63: *(top)* photo, H. Loebel for *Horizon* magazine, courtesy of New York Public Library
66-67: Conzett and Huber, Zurich
70: James B. Johnson, DPI
73: *(top)* Marlborough-Gerson Gallery, New York City; *(bottom)* Doris Bry
76-77: Malak, Miller Services Ltd.
80: Marlborough-Gerson Gallery, New York City
92-93: *Childcraft* photo
95: *(bottom)* James B. Johnson, DPI
96-97: *Horizon* magazine
98-99: © Nationalmuseum, Stockholm, Sweden
100: Syd Greenberg, DPI
102-103: © Smeets Lithographers, Weert, Netherlands
104: Barrett Gallagher
106: George Rodger, Magnum
108-109: *(top)* *Childcraft* photo; *(bottom left)* Dimitri Kessel, *Life* © Time Inc.; *(bottom right)* Seattle Center Department, City of Seattle
110: Jonas Dovydenas
115: Karl Milch
116: © New York Graphic Society Ltd., Greenwich, Conn.
125: Giraudon
127: Modern Art Selections, S.A., New York City
128-129: © William Garnett
130: © Toni Frissell
134: Giraudon
137: Helga Photo Studio, Inc.
140: Photographs Archive of the Austrian National Library
150-151: © Soho Gallery, London

152: Bob McCormack
153: Alinari from Art Reference Bureau
156-157: Ranson Photographers Ltd.
158: Bob McCormack
168-169: Carlo Bavagnoli, *Life* © Time Inc.
170: *Childcraft* photo by Robert Crandall
172: *Childcraft* photo by Robert Crandall
174: *Childcraft* photo from Il Libro Del Mondo, Milan, Italy
175: Harry N. Abrams, Inc.
180: Geoffrey Clements Photography
182-183: Courtesy of Hammer Galleries, New York City
184-185: Art Reference Bureau
190: Dorothy McLaughlin
192: E. Irving Blomstrann, New Britain, Conn.
194: Nat and Yanna Brandt, Photo Researchers
196-197: John Hill
203: G. D. Hackett
210: *(top)* Eric Pollitzer
212: Joachim Blauel
216: Ruth Orkin
218: *(left)* Time-Life Books © Time Inc.
219: *(top left)* *Childcraft* photo by Peter Gold; *(top right)* American Heritage Publishing Co., Inc.; *(bottom right)* Mexican Government Tourist Department
222: Annan Photo Features
224: Eric Schall, *Time* © Time Inc.
228: A. J. Wyatt
231: *Childcraft* photo
236: *Childcraft* photo by Robert Crandall
237: Alinari from Art Reference Bureau
239: Lincoln McCabe
246: Hugh Rogers, Monkmeyer
248: *(bottom left)* *Childcraft* photo by Rene Burri, Magnum; *(bottom right)* Frank Willett
250: *(left)* © Bijutsu Shuppan-sha, Tokyo, Japan
250: *(right)* Art Reference Bureau
251: Oscar Savio
256-257: *Childcraft* photos
261: Museum Color Slides Association
266-267: UNESCO, Laurenza
269: *(bottom left)* *Childcraft* photo by Jacqueline Mackay from Nancy Palmer
270: © Yousuf Karsh from Rapho Guillumette
271: *(top)* *Life* magazine
273: © The Frick Collection, New York City
278-279: *Childcraft* photos
280-281: Pictorial Parade

Heritage binding cover—*(left to right): (back)* University of Georgia, Il Libro Del Mondo, *Childcraft* photo, Field Enterprises Educational Corporation collection; *(spine)* Kunsthistorisches Museum, Vienna *; *(front)* *Childcraft* photo, Giorgio Calzolari from Ducal Palace, Mantua, Rene Burri, Magnum, Peter Gold from Mr. and Mrs. Michael Hoffner, Park Ridge, Illinois

Index of Artists

This index will help you find a work of art shown in this book if you know the name of the artist. The nationality of each artist is given in parentheses after his or her name. All titled works are in *italics*. The place where each work of art may be seen, the year it was done, and the medium used are given in the caption on the page indicated. Works of art shown in other volumes can be found through the General Index in Volume 15.